INTERNATIONAL PHOTO ALBUM
ATHENS

INTERNATIONAL PHOTO ALBUM
ATHENS
NICOLAI CANETTI & NICK MANLEY

PEEBLES PRESS
New York·London

First Published 1977 by
Peebles Press International, Inc.
10 Columbus Circle, New York, New York 10019

DESIGNED BY NICOLAI CANETTI

© 1977 Peebles Press International, Inc.
ISBN 0-672-52358-2
Library of Congress Catalog Card Number 77–76021

Photographs by Nicolai Canetti pages: 2, 8-9, 10, 11, 12-13, 14, 16, 17, 18, 19, 20, 21, 22, 23, 24-25, 26, 27, 29, 30, 31, 32, 33, 34, 35, 36, 39, 40-41, 42, 43, 44, 45, 46, 47, 48, 49, 50, 51, 52-53, 54, 55, 58, 59, 60, 64, 65, 67, 68, 69, 70, 71, 72-73, 74, 76, 78, 79, 80, 84, 85, 86, 87, 89, 91, 94, 96, 97, 101, 102, 103, 104, 105, 107, 108, 109, 110, 111, 115, 116, 118, 119, 121, 122, 123, 124, 125, 126, 127, 128, 129, 130, 131, 132, 136, 137, 138, 139, 140.

Photographs by Nick Manley pages: 15, 28, 37, 38, 56, 57, 61, 62-63, 66, 75, 77, 81, 82, 83, 88, 90, 92, 93, 95, 98, 99, 100, 106, 112, 113, 114, 117, 120, 126, 133, 134, 135, 141, 142.

Distributed by
The Bobbs-Merrill Co., Inc.
4300 West 62nd St., Indianapolis, Indiana 46268, U.S.A.
in the United States and Canada

Barrie & Jenkins
24 Highbury Crescent
London N5 1RX, England
in the U.K., Ireland, Australia, New Zealand and South Africa

Printed and bound in the United States of America

INTRODUCTION

Athens is the capital of the relatively modern state of Greece that won its independence from the Ottoman Empire only in 1834. Since then it has been the seat of monarchies, dictatorships and republics, but as early as 507 B.C. it was a democracy that was the very real foundation of the philosophical movement that is still very much alive in the world today. The city's origin is lost in myth. Legend tells us that it was named after the goddess Athena who sprang forth fully armed from Zeus's forehead. According to the same tradition it was she who gave the city the olive trees that are so abundant throughout the whole country.

Athens' history is still very much a part of today. The heart of the ancient city, the Acropolis, stands out proudly above the bustle of modern squares and buildings and not far away is another hill, the Areopagus or Hill of Mars, where Paul of Tarsus gave his famous sermon on the Unknown God. Right below the Acropolis is a theater built by Herod Atticus in 161 B.C. where the comedies of Aristophanes and the tragedies of Aeschylus are said to have been performed, and which is still very much in use.

If classical civilization, despite the wear of time and the vandalism of conquerors and thieves, has survived in stone, Christianity too has left its indelible mark not only on the character of the Greek people, but on the architecture of the city as well. Remnants of the Byzantine period can be seen all over the city, hidden behind modern office buildings or apartment houses. One of the oldest and most authentic examples of Byzantine influence is the tiny "old" cathedral which now services the small Russian Orthodox community.

Architecture can never be the heart of a city. Athens is much more than two-thousand-five-hundred years of stone and mortar. It is living and vibrant with the clear, almost tangible light of the Aegean. It pulsates with the noises of the Near East, mingling with the new sounds of the West. Its atmosphere is pervaded by the incense of the churches, the savour of spit-roasted baby lamb or fish frying, the musk and the spice of the markets and the perfume of flowers.

Most of all, Athens is people, a people filled with warmth and friendliness, a people whose word for stranger and guest, *xenos*, is the same. Athens is the Evzone and the shoeshine man, the ship-builder and the craftsman, the bouzouki musician and the sailor, the souvenir-vendor and the icon-painter, the bearded priest and the effervescent young student, the old matron selling her handmade shawl and the girl radical peddling the Communist newspaper.

Athens is light, perfume, music, history, but above all it is *philoxenia*—the love of strangers.

Carl Underhill Quinn

Athens, the eye of Greece, mother of arts
And eloquence, native to famous wits
Or hospitable, in her sweet recess,
City or suburban, studious walks and shades;
See there the olive grove of Academe,
Plato's retirement, where the Attic bird
Trills her thick-warbled notes the summer long.

—John Milton
PARADISE REGAINED

The Temple of the Parthenon designed and built by Ictinus, Callicrates and Phidias is set on the Acropolis, one of the hills that overlooks Athens, and is dedicated to the goddess Athena, the patron of the city. The Temple has been used throughout history by other religions as a place of worship—particularly by early Christian followers who converted it into a church and, later, by the Turks who turned it into a mosque from the seventeenth to the nineteenth century when they occupied Greece.

A Caryatid from the Erechtheum, an Ionic temple on the Acropolis, is one column in a series that has been sculpted in the images of beautiful priestesses to form the Porch of the Maidens. The Porch supports the marble roof of the Temple dedicated to the goddess Athena and god Poseidon, and completed during the last years of the Peloponnesian Wars (431-404 B.C.). It was to the west of the Erechtheum that Athena is said to have struck the surface of a rock from which the first olive tree sprang.

The Propylaea, the gateway to the Acropolis, was built in 437 B.C. of Pentelic marble by the
architect, Mnisicles, as a processional entrance. The Propylaea contains three parts: a
central entrance and two wings, one of which was used in ancient times as a painting gallery.

The Parthenon.

The Theater of Herod Atticus, also called the Odeion, on the south side of the Acropolis, was built in 161 B.C. Today, with a capacity to accommodate five thousand people, it houses the Athens Festival, a series each summer of open air performances of opera, ballet and concerts by Greek and foreign artists.

OPPOSITE PAGE: Statue around the area of the Stoa of Attalus.

The Temple of Hephaestus, better known today among the Greeks as the Theseion,
situated near the Agora, is one of the best preserved ancient temples in Greece.

The area around the Stoa of Attalus is in the northwest of Athens below the Acropolis near the Agora, which was the ancient city's commercial and civic center. The Stoa, or arcade, contained the market place, other shops and administrative buildings. Today, it has been completely reconstructed, serving as an archaeological museum.

The Propylaea.

Temple of the Olympian Zeus, also called the Olympeion, stands to the east of the Acropolis in the heart of Athens. The construction of the Temple, began under Pisistrates in 530 B.C., was not completed until 129 A.D. under the Roman Emperor Hadrian.

The Temple of Athena Nike, or the Temple of Wingless Victory, stands to the right of the Propylaea on the Acropolis. The small structure was built in the fifth century B.C. to commemorate the Greek victories over the Persians. The frieze of the Temple depicts scenes from these battles.

OPPOSITE PAGE: Hadrian's Arch was built by the Roman Emperor, Hadrian, to delineate the boundary between "the City of Theseus" and "the City of Hadrian" during the Roman occupation of Athens which began in 86 B.C.

View of Hadrian's Arch from a side street in the old part of Athens, called Plaka, which lies at the foot of the Acropolis.

The Tower of the Winds, built in the first century B.C. by the astronomer, Andronicus, is situated near the Acropolis. The octagonal edifice contains figures and inscriptions of the eight winds, and was intended originally to be used as a hydraulic clock for it includes a sun dial and weather vane. It is also known as the "Clock of Cyrrhistus."

The House of Parliament is located above Constitution Square. The nineteenth century neo-classic building, originally used as the Royal Palace, was designed by Bavarian architects whom King Otto brought to Athens, after Greece won her independence in 1834 from the Ottoman Empire, which occupied the country for almost four centuries. The newly liberated people appealed to the Bavarian royal line, the House of Wittelsbach, for a monarch because they had no native person with royal blood to succeed the Turks. At that point in European history, it was politically and socially important for a country to be headed by a leader from royal stock.

The lower part of the building, The Tomb of the Unknown Soldier, is a monument in honor of those who have died during the Greek War of Independence in 1821, and during the two World Wars.

Evzone Guard wearing the traditional Greek military uniform stands in front of The
Tomb of the Unknown Soldier

Legs of the Evzone Guards displaying part of the unique uniform they wear.

A busy commercial street in the center of Athens where one may find all types of fabrics including fine linens and laces—in the background, Kapnikarea, a tiny Byzantine church, the oldest in the city now used by a Russian Orthodox congregation.

View of Athens with the Plaka (the old quarter) in the foreground. In the distance, Lycabettus Hill with the Byzantine chapel of St. George at its summit. One may walk up or take the funicular to the top to eat in the restaurant as well as to enjoy the panoramic view of the city.

St. Catherine's Church, a "modern" church, in the Plaka, dating around one hundred years old.

Aghioi Theodoroi, an eleventh century Byzantine church which is the best preserved
of its kind in Athens, stands in the middle of a modern business district.

Commercial street with Kapnikarea in the background.

Agios Eleftherios, another tiny Byzantine church which is literally surrounded by towering modern buildings in the heart of Athens.

48

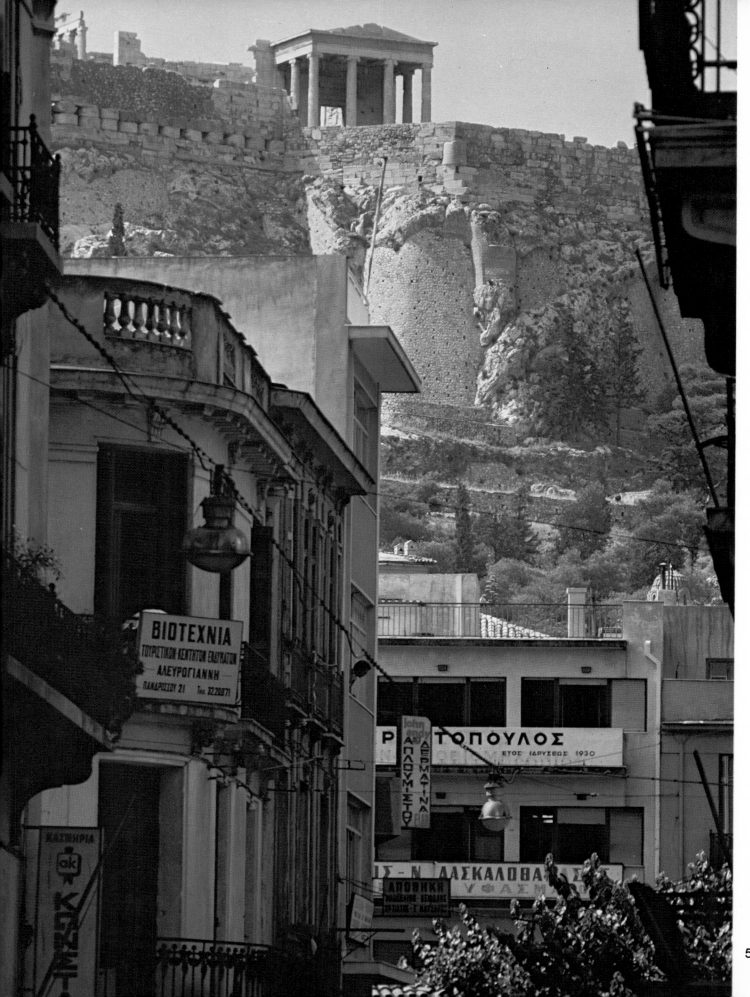

Elderly man with worry beads.

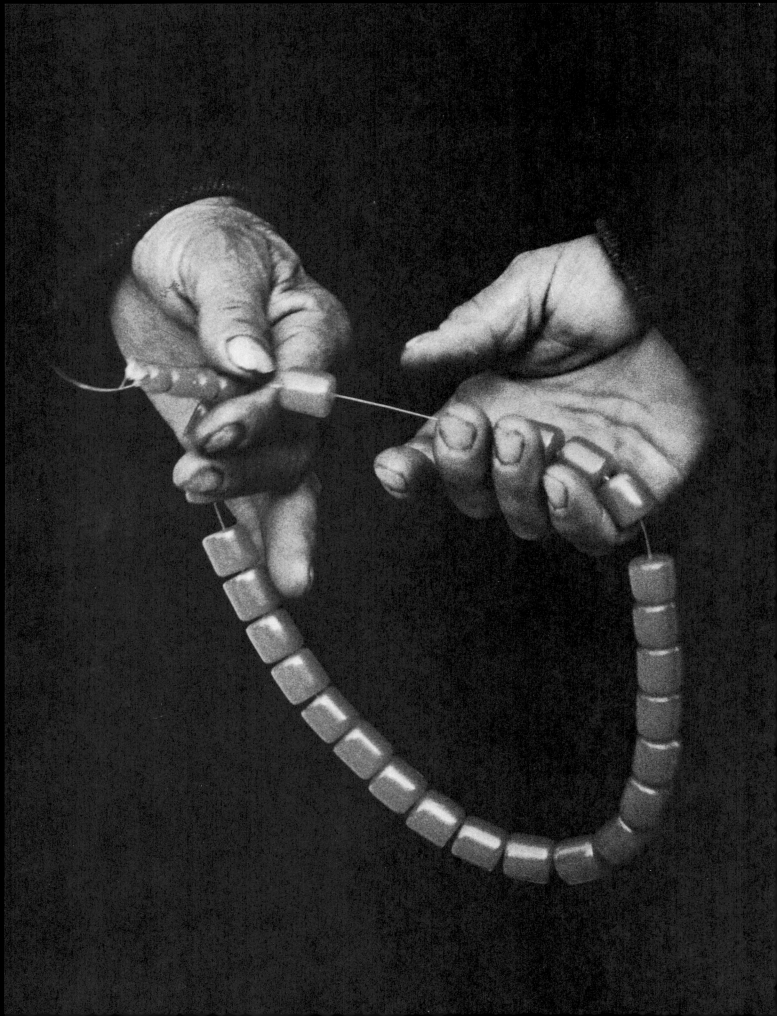

A shopkeeper in the Flea Market or Monastiraki, as it is called, named after the tenth century Byzantine church in the center of the main square of the Market. On Sunday mornings, particularly, Monastiraki offers shoppers a chance to find bargains in all wares from antiques and handicrafts to furniture and clothing.

A street in Monastiraki lined with stores selling antiques, traditional Greek embroidered blouses and skirts as well as brass ware.

Stores in Monastiraki.

Old peasant women selling handmade shawls in Monastiraki.

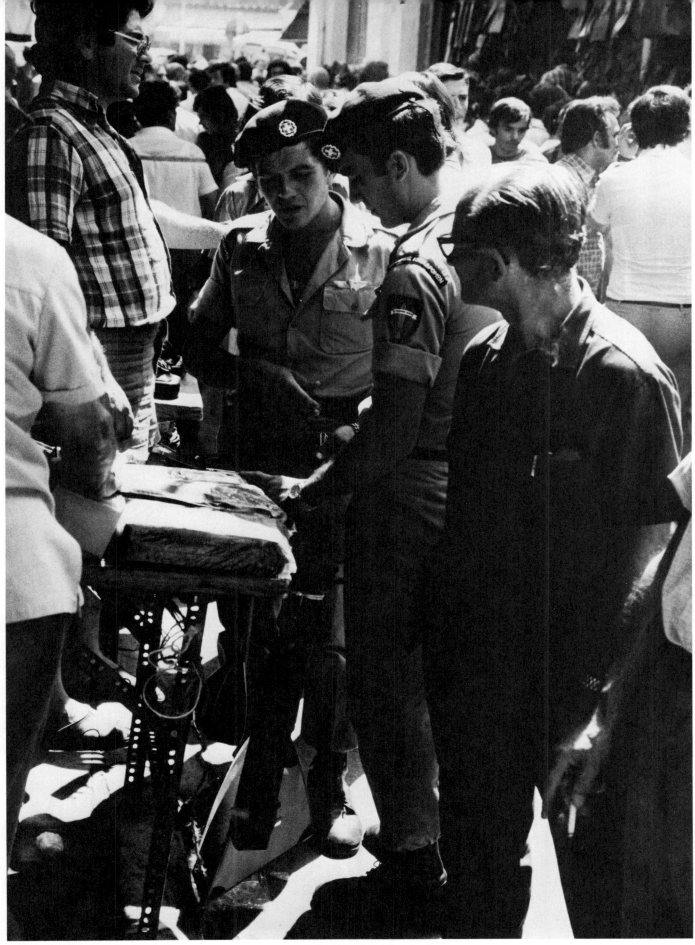

Greek soldiers In Monastiraki.

Shoe vendors displaying their merchandise on the street in Monastiraki.

Souvenirs, jewelry, brass ware and mattresses all in one store.

Old peasant woman selling handmade knitted shawls, sweaters, as well as other clothes.

A boutique having a sale in the fashionable shopping area near Constitution Square.

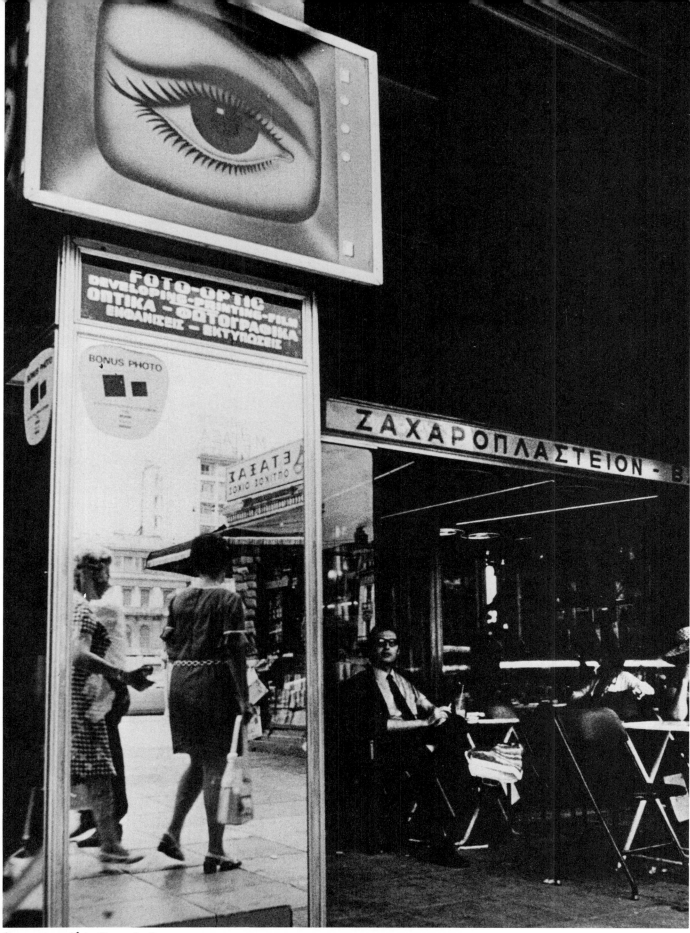

Open air café in Omonia Square.

Open air cafés in the Plaka.

Open air cafés around Constitution Square.

Open air cafés around Constitution Square.

Policeman directing traffic in downtown Athens during rush hour.

Constitution Square, also known as Syntagma Square, surrounded by elegant hotels, boutiques and stores as well as delightful open air cafés, is one of the most sophisticated parts of Athens.

Carriage driver in the Plaka.

Monastiraki.

View of Athens from the Kolonaki Square area.

View of Athens, the Plaka in the foreground. The government of Athens has issued a law preventing the building of highrises in the old quarter as an effort to preserve the charm and integrity of that section.

Repair shops in the downtown section of Athens near the factories and garages.

OPPOSITE PAGE: A meat market also in the downtown area.

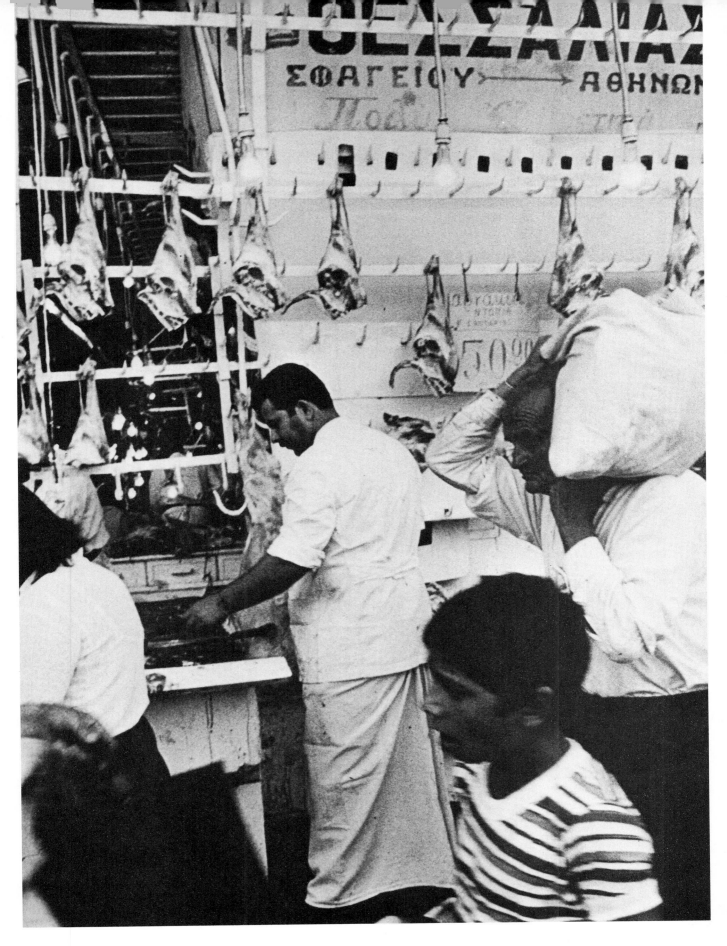

Coin dealer in the downtown area near the stock market. OPPOSITE PAGE: Vendor in Monastiraki.

Shopping in Monastiraki . . .

and in downtown Athens.

Almost all apartment buildings in Athens have terraces as does this one in the Plaka. It is quite usual to see people, primarily women, sitting on their terrace, conversing with their neighbor, reading, napping or doing some household chore like sewing.

Selling ice cream in Monastiraki.

Fruit and vegetable markets.

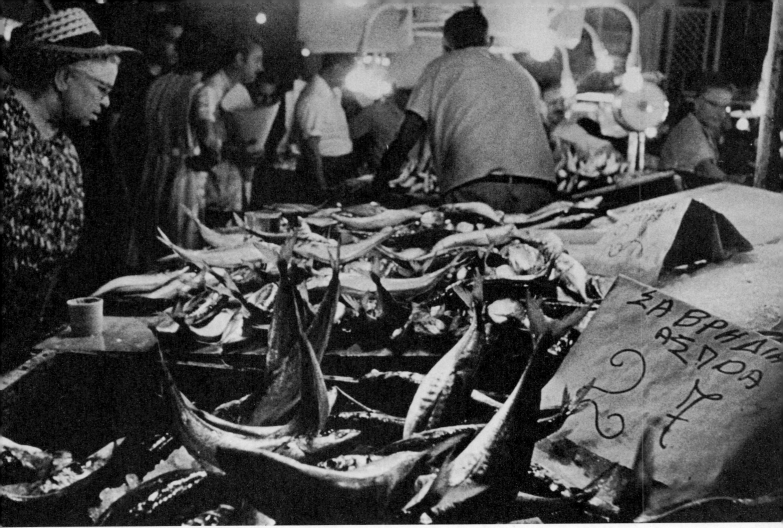

Indoor fish market near Omonia Square.

OPPOSITE PAGE: Priest in a butcher shop near Omonia Square.

Fruit and vegetable vendor.

Farmers and people who keep a garden often buy live poultry to raise, and sometimes, to breed and sell.

Woman standing in front of a bus stop after shopping near Constitution Square.

The hand truck is a common mode of transport in Athens.

Selling charcoaled corn-on-the-cob on the street in Athens is as popular and common as selling chestnuts on the street in New York, London or Paris.

Kiosk near Constitution Square where one may find newspapers, aspirin, worrybeads, postcards, candy, cigarettes, souvenirs . . . and even a telephone.

Shopkeeper in the downtown area of Athens.

Man selling lottery tickets. He grasps a wooden stick with slits to hold the tickets—a typical way in which lotteries are sold in Athens.

Man selling lottery tickets in front of one of the entrances to the garden surrounding
The House of Parliament.

Street vendor selling nuts in Monastiraki.

The women dressed in black are probably in mourning, although frequently older women in Greece wear dark clothing as a matter of course.

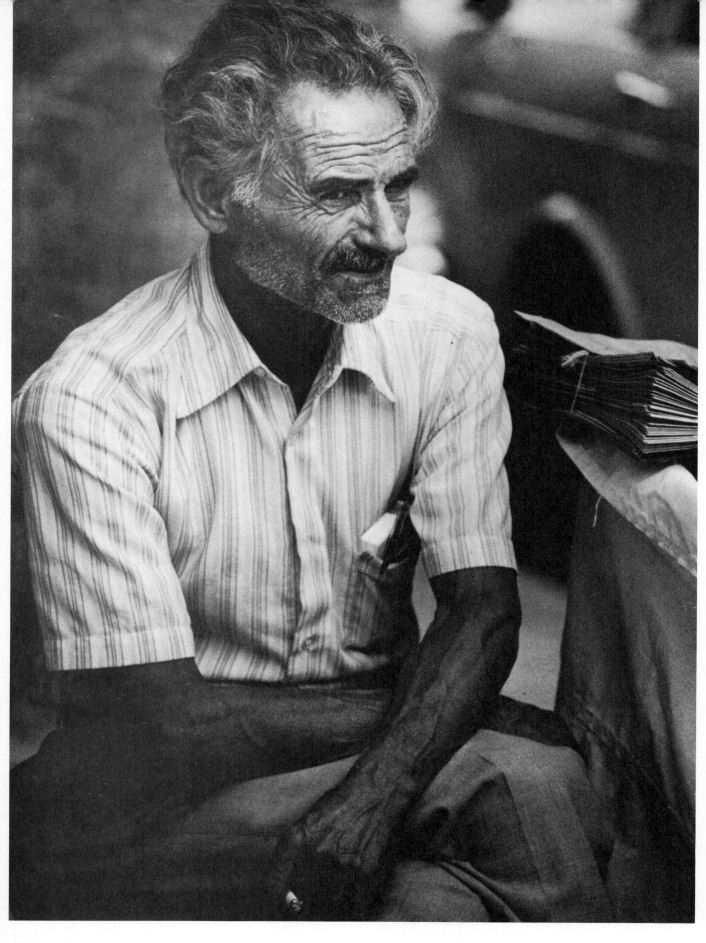

Man wearing a black scarf wrapped around his head in the traditional style from the island of Crete. The style is said to be reminiscent of the way ancient pirates wore their bandannas.

Priest waiting in front of a bus stop.

Priest carrying an evening paper which he just bought from a kiosk.

Young girls selling the communist newspaper, *The Leader*.

Selling shoes in Monastiraki.

LIST OF COLOR PHOTOGRAPHS